T0064176

Frozen Moments

Also by Uma:

- "***Home-coming***" – A translation of the original in Sri Lankan Tamil Katha, New Delhi
- "***The Man who Tamed Electricity***" – Article on Michael Faraday Children's Book Trust, New Delhi
- "***Home Away from Home***" – A short story in "The Rage of a New Ancestor" New Asian Writing, Thailand
- ***Script Practice (Hiragana & Katakana)*** Geetham Publications, Chennai
- "***Steve Jobs***" – Translation of Walter Isaacson's Exclusive Biography of Steve Jobs into Tamil (to be released shortly) Adaiyaalam Publishers, Trichy

Frozen Moments

Echoes from the Valleys of Life

UMA BALU

PARTRIDGE
A Penguin Random House Company

To order additional copies of this book, contact
Partridge India
000 800 10062 62
orders.india@partridgepublishing.com

www.partridgepublishing.com/india

Contents

To
This beautiful world

Even a thousand-mile journey
begins with the first step.
- Japanese proverb

Foreword

What distinguishes between Poetry and Prose as two different genres of literary expression is the basic appeal of moments of creativity. To quote William Wordsworth, "Poetry takes its origin in emotion recollected in tranquility." S.T. Coleridge, on the other hand, describes poetry as a chamber of mysticism from whose ivory towers he could fancy thoughts metaphysical. Byron saw poetry as a very justification for his passionate intoxication with his sensual pleasures - a constant source of inspiration to him. To Shelley, poetry was an occasion for the "sweetest songs that tell us of our saddest thoughts". Not to be left far behind, John Keats — that master craftsman who revived the memories of The Poet's Poet — defines poetry in particular and arts in general: "Beauty is truth and truth, beauty/ That's all you need to know." While the appeal is to our emotional response, prose is starkly rational, logical, coherent - a discourse that reminds you of a long goods train meandering over the Trans-Siberian mountains. Poetry, on the other hand, is a journey into the mystic Himalayas - from whichever col you choose your climb. One cloys your senses whilst the other thrills your sensibilities.

In the unforgettable lines of Uma's "Frozen Moments", you will never get cloyed or satiated with the "shared experiences". She has gone through life's varied moments of joys, ecstacies,

13

sorrows and tragedies with utmost equanimity and her personal experiences are presented in distilled capsules in her own choice diction that is highly suggestive of her depth of feeling. Was it George Eliot who wished that "Great art lies in concealing art"? If that is the criteria of judging greatness of artistic quality, then these frozen moments are definitely milestones of simple but enduring, alluring poetic recollections.

What makes Frozen Moments all the more alluring is the fact that these emotions transcend a monolinguistic experience. Uma being born with the DNA of analytically sound techniques of Pedagogy, carries on her family traits to an exemplary level of multi-linguistic expression. Being a linguist much more than a polyglot, she sails the day through her inspirational portrayal of great moments in everyone's life. Having been a promising daughter to her gifted parents, a dutiful wife to her charming husband and a doting mother to her beloved boys through every thick and thin, Uma has rolled out universality through her poetic creations.

Browse, dip and soak yourself in these "moments" - maybe you would discover a new You and create your own moments that will "thaw" against hers. That is the kind of inspiration that truly great creative artists can generate!

May her tribe increase!

Dr. Vridhachalempillay Subramaniam.,
UNESCO Fellow on Pedagogy
E-mail: drvsubramaniam@gmail.com
Mobile: 94440 42771

Preface

Life is a great teacher…
Experiences chisel our personality and character…
Somewhere on the way, thoughts play magic…
Transforming dull, routine moments into creative ones…
Words and expressions emerge from nowhere…
They just fall into place, and blend naturally
into an exquisite piece of art…
Behind every poem of mine –
there is a special moment…
a special person too…
"Frozen Moments" belongs to them…

Uma

A Universal Message

His Holiness Sri Sankaracharya of Kanchi

Learn the language of love that conquers hearts...
See others as mirrors, reflecting yourself...
Weed away jealousy and rivalry...
Seek not what doesn't belong to you...

Earth, our Mother, is bountiful and benevolent...
God, our Father, is merciful and lenient...
O mankind, practice the principles of humility,
generosity and magnanimity...
May humanity be blessed with prosperity!

Part I

Inspirations

The story of a seed

A transformation from a simple existence to a mighty presence...some people enter your life and make no difference..some others work wonders in every sense!

Once upon a time...
there was a seed...
a marvellous creation of nature...
a vision of the future...

it lay there...
with no one to care...
amidst dust and dry leaves...

tossed by the wind...
scorched by the sun...
waiting... and longing...
for those divine hands unseen...

days, months and years passed by...
it still lay there...thinking...
to live or to die...

it was a warm summer day...
a clear blue sky...
nothing so special...
nothing so different...

slow, but sure...
the great moment arrived...

nature waved her magic wand...
a whiff of cool breeze...
grey clouds from nowhere...
and the first drops of... rain!

birds burst into song...
the mountains echoed...
the trees quivered in delight...
celebration of joy...everywhere...

the seed wondered...
what is happening to me...
this strange feeling...
the smell of fresh earth...
the first signs of life...
the dawn of a new beginning?

time... the great traveller...
took gentle strides...

and the seed...
it still lay there...
somewhere, deep within -
it felt a gentle touch...

each moment it grew...
till one lovely day...
when a tiny voice called:
"I want to see this beautiful world!"

it was a leaf...
so delicate... so tender...
fresh and vibrant...
full of life...

the seed listened...

was it God's voice?
a message so meaningful...
worth all the waiting...

before it knew...
its crusty, brown shell opened...
to the touch of love...
a transformation!

years from now...
it shall grow...
into a mighty tree...
reaching to the skies...

spreading its branches wide...
laden with fruit...
holding many a seed...

each with a destiny...
a story to call its own...

every road has its destination...
every life, its purpose...
find the heart that cares...
the shoulders that support...
the arms that welcome...

and discover the real YOU...

Small is beautiful

The simple delights of life are missed in the pusuit of material belongings.. This poem rediscovers them.

When you say a sweet word
The smile that adorns my face –
That's my most precious jewel..

When your arms wring around my shoulders
The pride that rivals a queen –
That's my grandest robe..

When we recall a funny moment
The laughter that fills our hearts –
That's my boundless wealth..

When in pangs of hunger
The bowl of saltless gruel we share –
That's my lavish dinner..

When we bask in the warmth of our thoughts
Under the starlit sky
On the cold, hard ground –
That's my cosy bed..

When you sing for me
In that magical voice, I forget myself;
That's the music of my life..

When we walk barefoot, hand in hand
Even miles seem a few steps;
Your shadow is my shade..

On a special day
Trying to open your fingers one by one
To find a tiny pebble on that soft palm -
Bathed in love..
That's my most cherished gift..

That golden heart of yours
Where I live forever
Is my heavenly abode..

Little acts of love
Fill life to the brim..

The richest of treasures
Are the easiest to find;
The simplest of pleasures
Are of the rarest kind..

If I could fly

**An attempt to capture a child's fertile imagination..
The words had to be expressive, yet simple**.

If I could fly
I would love to be a kite
Watching the children's faces
Filled with delight..

If I could fly
I would love to be a bird
Diving into the valleys
Soaring into the skies..

If I could fly
I would love to be a bubble
Clear as a crystal
Coloured as the rainbow..

Fork, knife and spoon

(a dialogue)

A **funny dialogue between unusual characters.**

Spoon: See, how softly I scoop food and carry it to the mouth...

Look at you... pricking all the time... with those sharp teeth...

Fork: Ha ha, no use being jealous...

Spoon: And that wonderful friend of yours – the knife - born to cut...

Fork: Oh yes, if he stops cutting and I stop pricking, what is there for you to scoop???

Butterfly and Flower

A dialogue between a butterfly and flower, bringing out the best qualities in them and also their deep appreciation for each other.

It's a lovely morning...
The earth looks so green...
With the sun's mild warmth...
And the wind's soft music...

"O little flower...
With that bright, cheerful smile...
Shall I rest my tired wings
On your petals for a while?"

"O beautiful butterfly...
With that subtle grace...
My petals shall offer you comfort
And my honey shall quench your thirst"

"O delicate flower...
I see thorns around you...
But still you remain unharmed
Ever fresh and new..."

"O gentle butterfly...
Life is a game...

The strong survive by their power...
The weak by their will..."

"O charming flower...
You are the symbol of beauty...
To this ever-changing world
You are a gift of nature"

"O lovely butterfly...
You are the symbol of freedom...
Like me, you make a million friends...
A delightful journey that never ends!"

Miss Mickey

A casual visit to the beach leads to a funny situation which later becomes a nightmare..finally, things take an unusual twist..

Miss Mickey went to the sea
And sat with sand heaped upto her knee
Everything was so lovely
Till there came a bumble-bee..

Over her head
It went - round and round;
She swat it dead
And it fell to the ground

Then a fly came buzzing by
And sat on Miss. Mickey's left eye
She raised her hand and gave it a slap -
Pop, pop... it fell on her lap!

Buzzing flies and bumble-bees
Miss.Mickey was no more at ease
Swishing and brushing all the time
Odd enough for my little rhyme!

Back home at last, she went to bed
Trying to cool her aching head

She closed her eyes, hoping to sleep
Not aware of the nightmare-in-keep...

Just then she heard a small, faint buzz...
The louder it grew, into a noisy whizz...
Bees and flies, on her legs and arms
Not one or two, but swarms and swarms!

She screamed in fright... now what to do...
There was no way out, not even a clue...
Groping around, she grasped something...
She had found the link, little knowing...

It was a bottle, round and green
Two handles and a spout between
Down there, little drops of wine
Even in dark, with a sparkle and shine!
In her panic, she let it fall
Out flew a fly, so small...
And then a big, fat bumble bee
So happy that it was free!

Buzzes and whizzes.. on and on..
Bees and flies, all were gone!

Lo and behold...
There she lay...
A dream so cold
On a summer day!

Marvel, man-made

A **child's imagination - personifying the computer and highlighting its evolution.**

Hello, Mr. Computer!
You are a man-made wonder!

You see with a camera
You show with a monitor
You think with a CPU
You write with a keyboard
And you travel on a mouse!
You sing, draw and paint
You also entertain!

You were big earlier..
And grew smaller and smaller..
Some day in the future
I may hold you on my finger!

Cups and slips

An extremely busy colleague trying desperately to finish his cup of hot coffee amidst a never-ending trail of phone calls…Finally he made it!

There's many a slip
Between the cup and the lip;
And many a trip
After each little sip;
When, at last
The cup meets the lip
It ends in a happy, happy sip.
No more trips – only sips
Now where are those slips
Between the cup and the lip?

Romance on a rainy day

Rainclouds and drizzles always fill the air with
romance and childish delight..

The fresh scent of soil after a drizzle...

Raindrops that shine like jewels on the fresh, green
leaves...

Sharing an umbrella and each taking care that the other
doesn't get wet...

Going for a walk on the not-so-crowded road, enjoying
the light drizzle, hand-in-hand...

Braving the flooded road, splashing through the muddy
water, competing with kids...

Dancing on the wet green grass, forgetting all worries, not
caring even if others think you've gone crazy, laughter that
brings out all the happiness within the heart...

Off to school, college or classes - especially when parents
lovingly advise you not to, for fear of catching a bad cold...

Friendship

Something so special, it can't be defined enough..

A friend is ...
One who shares your joy as well as sorrow...
One who need not be near you, but still make his/her presence felt...
One who never misunderstands you...
One who reads your mind before you speak...
One who has the right to check you when you commit a mistake...
One who can capture the change in mood from even a simple 'Hi!'
I remember...
My friend always used to start a chat with Hi!!!!!!
That day it was just Hi
See the difference!
The first finger to wipe away your tears...
The first shoulder to lighten a heavy heart...
Lucky are those who have a spouse as a friend...
Luckier, those who have a friend as a spouse!

On your footsteps

Friends are always special. They sail us through the ups and downs of life, hold us together by their wise counsel and cheer us by their delightful company..

Fresh raindrops
On the parched earth…
Whiffs of cool breeze
In the scorching desert…

Lively white waves
On the silent, blue sea…
An understanding friend
In a meaningless life…

Life was a desert
Till I found the oasis that was you…
When the sun scorched from above
Your trees gave me shade…

When my throat was parched
Your springs quenched my thirst…
When my tired legs stumbled
Your cool breeze gave them comfort…

O dear…
Is there anything in this world –
That I can do for you?

Let me be your shadow
Wherever you go…

Let me be your reflection
To share your every emotion…

Let me be your wings
When you realize your dream…

Lifetimes forever
Yours I shall remain…
To cheer you –
Comfort you –
Love you –
And live with you…

Silence

Sometimes silence speaks louder than words..the heart longs for the revival of relationship..

Like a puzzle...
to which there is no answer...
Like a dark cloud...
which doesn't clear away...
Like a wall...
that blocks the view...
Your silence hurts.

Once I felt transformed...
from a knotty bud to a bright blossom...
from a crusty coccoon to a beautiful butterfly...
happy and singing...
with a cheerful heart...
my delight echoed in your song too...
in that magical voice, all my worries vanished...
when am I going to hear that again...

Should that happiness last...
Should the butterfly live...
Should the flower smile...
or should everything be engulfed again

in a hard, rocky shell -
that would never open for life?

Ask your heart -
And answer..

Fire festival

A moody day warmed up by expressions that lift the spirits - to a celebration!

Yesterday was the best of all...
Began with a very soft 'aalaap'...
followed by teasers and sparklers
(occasional compliments) -
for a slight warming up...

A sudden whiff of breeze...
and it just caught fire!
poetry, puns and praises
with a generous spicing of
dosas, romali rotis and potatoes..
burners galore!

By and by...
a magical transformation...
monsoons arrived...
the flames cooled down...
stars lit the night sky...

The Fire Festival!

Creativity

I had once sent an entry to a competition. It won a special prize. When the anthology of prize-winning entries was about to be published, I received a rejection letter saying I had compiled the article by copy-pasting information from various sources. I explained that it was not just an arbitrary collection of info, but a well-planned and sequential presentation in my original style. They were convinced and with a few finishing touches, it was accepted! This poem expresses my feelings on receiving their letter..

When you see those glossy yards
Whom do you admire –
The worm's silk or the weaver's skill?

A patch is just a patch -
Worth nothing;
Deft hands can match
And create –
Just anything!

Straws, sticks and leaves
Lying far apart…

A bird's instinct transforms them
Into a delicate work of art!

Words belong to everyone –
A masterpiece, only to one!

Mulberry leaves

Once I received an animated greeting card. It had
bright green leaves swaying softly. A few seconds later
a cute worm crawled by - with big, round eyes wide
open and a warm smile, it said "Hello!" It reminded
me of a mulberry worm and its creative instincts..

I am a little worm
Somewhere, within me
Lies hidden, a loom;

Leaf after leaf –
Of a bright, glossy green
I munch, day by day –
Adding to the sheen;

Months pass by –
And it's time to rest;
No food, only sleep
In my cozy, little nest;

One fine morning
I wake up from my sulk;
Spinning yards and yards
Of the finest silk;

Whenever you wear
That gorgeous saree
Whenever you wear
That splendid dhoti
Think of its weaver –
The worm, that was ME!

Born to win

Unity in diversity – let's make India proud!

There was an olden time
When India saw its best..

Merchants crossed the seas,
Scholars pursued knowledge;
Kings ruled the country –
And the rest had their choice..

Yet, one supported the other
In striving for the better;
Or else, who was the great Maurya –
Without the cunning Chanakya?

Akbar believed in harmony;
He was loved by his people..
The Rajputs gave him a 'Biwi'
And also his favourite, Birbal!

Asoka became Great with ease –
For that, he paid too high a price;
It was a Buddhist monk's advice
That brought his mind back to peace..

Politics becomes a religion
When welfare is its sole aim;
Hindus, Muslims and Christians
Are then no different, but the same..

Religion becomes politics
When it extends from the self towards society;
Crossing all its limits –
To spread goodwill, peace and piety.

Water, water everywhere

Japanese presence in India is steadily increasing day by day. During the floods, Chennai's roads were in a total mess. This poem describes a Japanese view of the situation.

Water, water everywhere
Not a drop to drink;
Garbage, garbage everywhere
Adding to the stink;

MM san, JJ san
Now it's time to think;
Chennai is a vital link –
Do not let it sink!

Destination

The last day at work..the future seemed so bleak.. words of comfort and motivation that came from a friend – the desperate need of the moment..

Soar, soar above –
Aiming your eyes;
Determined –
To conquer the skies;

There lie ahead
Wonderful things;
Gear up
And spread your wings;

Like the swift, delicate arrow
Powered by the mighty bow;
Zoom forth, be it day or dark –
Never stop, till you reach your mark!

Dust that settle may
Is nothing but a shell;
Just cast it away
And break the spell!

Uma Balu

When the heart speaks

Ghazals speak a lot about the heart.. my little ghazal!

O, little heart…
With your soft lub-dub
The body lives;
With your subtle language
The world lives.

Between the lines

Balancing the mind and heart is a skill indeed!

Your mind is wider than the sea, dear…
And your heart, deeper;
Which one do you want me to read?

If it is the mind,
Teach mine – I can learn;
If it is the heart,
Touch mine, I can feel…

Fountain of love

Holding a poet's pen.. capturing the special moment - in a poem!

Not just a pen –
But an exquisite creation of nature
That could pour forth
A thousand stories of love..

An eternal fountain
Each drop of ink
Delicately woven –
Into a string of pearls..

Blessed was I..
To hold that marvel
In my very own hands;
A moment so cherishable
For lifetimes to come..

Rain tree

Rain spells romance in Indian hearts..

A summer shower...
dark clouds chasing away the humid weather...
the green canopy, like a giant umbrella...
thick foliage... glistening raindrops...
doves seeking shelter from the rain...
hidden among the leaves, the koels burst into song...
their parched throats quenching thirst to the fill...
romance in the air...
a cool, gentle breeze...
whistles through the treetop...
the leaves rattle...
letting the raindrops fall...
drenched and delighted, the doves flutter...
there... in the distance...
against the grayish blue sky...
in all its colourful glory...
Cupid's rainbow.

Avatars

To father, a special person in life.. a multi-faceted personality gifted with rare talent.. comments and compliments at the appropriate moments..

A thousand mile journey begins with the first step...
mine too...and a beautiful beginning indeed...
drifting back into time...
a wonderful team...hand in hand...
miles apart... yet close to heart...
what all we shared...
work, wisdom, wishes..even worries...
I appreciate you...

Seasons keep changing...
situations too...
castles vanished into thin air...
future seemed bleak...
but...
a ray of hope remained...
I thank you...

People are born...
and birthdays celebrated...
but we were different...
we celebrated birthdays...
and were born again...

as special people...
I welcome you...

World's greatest dad...
and his wonderful family...
like fragrant flowers strung into a festoon...
by the chain of love...
I adore you...

Within the heart, somewhere...
there lie deep thoughts, wanting to share...
like birds of a flock...
reflections in water...
we saw one in another...
I admire you...

Love, they say, is blind...
Here is one..
blind with passion...
roaming the earth, sea and sky...
with his classic romance...
I love you...

Eyes spitting fire...
armed with knives...
horns to kill...
ropes to strangle...
I challenge you...

Weaving dreams into reality...
casting fantasy into form...
illusions into illustrations...
anything from nothing...
I applaud you...

O epitome of patience…
I worship YOU!

A bird story

What the true heart seeks..

In the lofty mountains, lived a beautiful bird...
She used to fly happily, singing her heart's song, enjoying the wild nature around...

Once she happened to meet a bird from the plains...
Cheerful, lively, happy-go-lucky, adventurous....
They were so different, yet found so much to share...

The bird from the plains told her, "It is nice to live in the lofty mountains... but there is a whole world beyond... Come along, discover its secrets, enjoy its beauty and make your life more meaningful..."

The mountain bird agreed and flew to the plains with her companion...
They fluttered around happily, singing, laughing and playing...

One day, they came across a cage.. a golden one, shining in the bright sun...
The bird from the plains said, "Come, let's enter and see... it looks great!"
But the mountain bird kept silent...

Then she said, "Dear friend, it indeed looks great, but I sense danger... it takes just a moment to enter... but once we do, we are trapped for life... instead, take me to your nest... the warmth of your nest, the comfort of your home, the company of your family and the constant companionship of yours... that is what I want... clip off my wings so that I never fly back to the lofty mountains, I don't mind... I shall stay on with you for ever... but never, never into this golden trap, my dearest friend..."

Lost years

Hard experiences strengthen the spirit…this poem appreciates a woman's determination to step on failures to reach the throne of success..

Remember?

There was a time –
sweet nothings went on without care..
now even a moment of yours is too busy to spare..

I wished for a home..
and got a house..

I longed for warmth..
You gave me a blanket..

Thanks for the pillows too..
Silent company, sharing my wet dreams..

Once you wrote a letter-
On a crumpled paper, in a scribbled hand..
Snatching those moments while waiting for the train..
Now there are forwarded messages for me to read and enjoy..

Your world has changed..
And drifted apart..
far too distant to listen to my heart..

Responsibility
Leans heavily on me..
yet, passing every while
with a mask of smile..

Hobbies have become
means of income..
in this life of haste and hurry
even a whiff of cool breeze is luxury..

Patience and perseverence
my spirit adorn..
Waiting in hope..
for a fresh, new dawn..

Wings of Freedom

To hell with those limits...
deadlines that spoil quality...
metres that block imagination..
frames that compress the landscape...
principles that cripple the journey of life..

duty and responsibility
are chains, too..
iron is burden..
but love, a bond..

transplant a seedling..
it can thrive in alien soil..
uprooting a banyan..
with roots and branches
spread far and wide..
and talking of survival?
suicide is a better option.

My mask dons a smile..
concealing the pain and tears..
You just took the smile for granted..

I can't imagine myself
ringing the bell
waiting for you
to open the door -
with that frown.

rules last till broken..
and change with the game
decisions last forever
they remain the same

My world is vast..
a million arms to embrace
a million faces to smile
and a million hearts to love..

wow..
the precious first step
towards recovering my lost years...

Into that world of freedom, my Father,
let my spirits awake!

Mistaken Identity

A lifetime taken for granted..
Ignited by indifference,
Charged by complaints..
Fuelled by frustrations..
Tormented by tears..
Wounded by words..

Things my very own –
Coveted without my permission
Or cast away, without my knowledge..

Strengths ignored..
Weaknesses exploited..
Sentiments hurt..
Dreams disturbed..

Worthless..

Like –
a dustbin..
a waste basket..
a dump yard..

How long can
the mighty waters be harnessed..
the raging volcano be suppressed..
the stormy skies be silenced..

Alive from the ashes..
Evolved from the elements..
Metamorphosis stranger than magic..
A total transformation.

Moments blessed with love..
Calm, compassion, caring and sharing..
Romance, understanding, togetherness and bonding..

Like -
a flower vase..
a spring garden..
a valley of blossoms..

Chewing Gum

The trees bled
in white trickles..

from the boiled sap
was born -
Chicle..

Sweet tongue twister
of those ancient tribes

Cows -
facing competition..
Thanks to Wrigley!

Tamil

Manaiyaa? Manamaa?

Manaiyadi saasthiram
Therinthavarkalukkellaam
Manathin saasthiram
Purinthuviduvathillai..

Paasamum banthamum koodap
Panaththirku baliyaakum kaalam..
Pattaakkalukkum paththirangalukkum pazhakiya kankal
Vaazhkkaiyaiye vilaipesum kolam..

Verodu pariththeduththu
Veridaththil nattuvittu
Vedikkai paarkkum manitharkal..
Ithai maram kooda erkaathu..
Manam erkumaa?

Nizhalendru ilaippaarinaal
Nagarnthu sendruvidum..
Kooraiyendru kannayarnthaal
Kuzhithondip puthaiththuvidum..

Karkaalaththil kooda illai
Inthak kalnenjam;
Tharkaalaththil theda,
"Illai" endra sol minjum..

(Translation)

Those who know the science of construction
May not understand the science of the heart..

It is an age of money
That enslaves love and bonding
Eyes that have got used to plots and bonds
now put up even lives for sale..

Uprooting and planting in alien soil..
For today's men, it's a game..
What even a tree can't accept..
How will the heart tolerate?

While I rest under the shade,
It moves away..
If I take it for a roof,
I crashes, burying me whole..

Even the Stone Age would not have seen
Hearts so hard..
Well, look for one now..
All you'll find is "NO"

Puthiya vidiyalai nokki

Vaazhkkaip payanaththil
nee paadangal pothiththaai
aasaanaai alla;
arakkanaai..

Enge pokiren..
eppothu sendradaiven..
ethuvum theriyavillai..

Aanaal..
eppadi endra kelvikku mattum
aayiram vidaikalundu..

Kukaikkul poottivaiththu
kaaval kaaththirunthaai..
kaikaal theya oornthu
velivarak kattrukkonden..

Thavazhnthavalukku aasaikaatti
engith thavikkavaiththaai;
un kaiyaik kurivaiththu
thalainimirak katrukkonden..

Keezhe thallivittaai;
kilarnthezhak katrukkonden..

Pinnaal thuraththivanthaai;
odak katrukkonden..

Neeril thallivittaai;
neenthak katrukkonden..

Mukattilirunthu uruttivittaai;
malaiyerak katrukkonden..

Kattip pottuvittu
kaikottich chiriththaai;
vittuth therikkumvarai
thimirak katrukkonden..

Ini ..

En paathai thodangum..
en payanam thodarum..

Puthiya vidiyalai nokki..

(Translation)

During the journey of life
You taught me lessons;
not as a teacher –
as a torturer..

Where am I going?
when will I reach?
I know not..

But -

If you ask me how,
I have a thousand answers..

You shut me inside a cave
and stood guarding at the entrance;
I crawled, with bruised hands and feet..
and learnt to emerge..

As I crawled out, you held things aloft
making me long in desire..
I watched those hands
and learnt to aim high..

You pushed me to the ground;
and I learnt to spring forth..

You chased me;
and I learnt to run..

You cast me into the waters;
and I learnt to swim..

You rolled me down the hill;
and I learnt to climb..

You bound my hands and feet
And clapped in glee..
Wriggling with all my might
I learnt to break free..

From now on..

My path shall begin..
My journey shall continue..

Towards a new dawn..

Part II

My "Beautiful Mistakes"

Dedicated with fondest love to
Mrs. Elfriede Malten
("Oma")

The story behind this title

There was one student from Germany – Thomas Malten. He had come to learn Tamil at Annamalai University, where my father, Dr. R. Ramachandran, was Reader in Mathematics. During one of his trips, he brought his mother, **Mrs. Elfriede Malten**, *along. She did not feel comfortable with English and I was desperately looking for a way to communicate with her. Finally, we made it - using our bilingual dictionaries!*

That was just the beginning. Soon, we started writing to each other and I thoroughly enjoyed the exercise! Once her birthday was round the corner - this time I wanted to write a special letter and requested Thomas to check the grammar. He read it and smiled: "Uma, you are an indefatigable writer of letters in the most **beautiful** *German… it is those* **mistakes** *that make it all the more delightful to read…I will not spoil it!"*

Golden words – etched in my memory…

So, here they are.. my 'beautiful mistakes' – carefully preserved!

Acknowledgements
Dr. Thomas Malten
Institute of Indology and Tamil Studies
Cologne University

German

Die Musiker von Bremen

My all-time favourite - from Grimm's Fairy Tales.

Wir sind vier Freunden
Die Musiker von Bremen

"Ich bin der Hund"
"Ich bin die Katze"
"Ich bin der Hahn"
"Und Ich bin der Esel"

Wir essen, wir trinken
Und schlafen zusammen;
Wir sind vier Freunden -
Die Musiker von Bremen

(Translation)

The musicians of Bremen

We are four friends
The musicians of Bremen

"I am the dog"
"I am the cat"
"I am the rooster"
"And I am the donkey"

We eat, we drink
and sleep together
We are four friends
The musicians of Bremen

Was ist denn los?

Swarna was my German teacher. Her classes were so lively and we immensely enjoyed it. Once she was unusually silent and a bit upset too – because we did not complete our homework.. it was too much of a contrast for me and an inspiration for this poem.

O, liebe Swarna!
Was ist denn los?
Du siehst aus was anders –
Ganz seriös!

Das herzlichen Lachen
Und freundlichen Augen
Die uns glücklich machen -
Wo sind sie gegangen?

Rechzeitig kommen -
Fleissig arbeiten -
Fliessend zu sprechen -
Hausaufgabe zu machen…

Wir wunschen alle;
Leider konnten wir nur wenige..
Verstehst du bitte..
Bleib nicht so böse!

Ein Sonne im Himmel
Gibt der ganzen Erde Licht
Eine Swarna vor der Tafel
Macht ein schönen Unterricht!

Heute – geht es weg
Morgen – kommt es bald;
Hoffen wir eine Swarna
Glanzend wie Gold!

(Translation)

What happened?

Oh dear Swarna
What happened?
You look so different –
So serious!

That hearty laughter
And those friendly eyes
That make us so happy –
Where have they gone?

Reaching on time
Working hard
Speaking fluently
Doing homework –

We too wish them all..
But were able to do only a little..
Please try to understand
Don't be so angry..

A sun in the sky
Lights up the whole earth
A Swarna before the blackboard
Livens up the whole class!

Today is passing by
Tomorrow will arrive soon
We hope for a Swarna
Dazzling as gold!

Indien – mein schönes Land

Our German class had students from different countries – a mini version of multi-lingual, multi-cultural India! Unity in diversity – a different context.

Ich wohne in ein schönes Land
Das sehr liebt – fast jemand
Wir bauen zwischen uns
Keine Wand;
Und gehen immer vor
Hand in Hand

Wann man etwas spricht
Und wir verstehen nicht
Gibt es keine Licht
In eine Unterricht

So bitte tun Sie
Ihre beste Pflicht
Das macht süßer als
Eine gute Gesicht!

Ich bin in Indien geboren
Wo kann man nie sich verloren
Vergessen Sie bitte, alle Sorgen
Es gibt immer einen guten Morgen!

(Translation)

I live in a beautiful country
That everyone loves..
We build no walls between
And always go hand in hand

When one says something
And we don't understand
There is no liveliness
in a classroom..

So, please
try your best
To make it sweeter..
than just a good face

I am born in India
Where one never gets lost
Please forget all your cares..
There is always a good morning!

French

Japon

My presentation for our classroom project at **Allaiance Francaise de Madras.**

Je suis Akito, je suis Japonais
Je presente vous, notre pays
Il y a quatre, grandes illes;
Les petites, numerouse – plus ses mille!

Rouge et blanc – c'est notre drapeau
Vert et bleu – c'est un land tres beau

Nous avons une culture speciale
Et modern et aussi traditionelle!

"Kimono" – s'appelle notre vetement
Plein de dessin, trop charmant!

Est-ce que vous ave regarde "Sumo"?
C'est notre sport – tres grand, tres gros!

Nous aimons les fleurs et la musique
Il fait une atmosphere unique!

Nous adorons les fruits de la mer
Mais monger a Japan – c'est vraiment cher!

Donnez-vous nous une
Feuille de papier
Nous pouvons creater
Un monde de votre cahier!

Quelque chose quand vous etes en vacance
Visite-vous Japon – bon chance!

(Translation)

I am Akito, I am Japanese
Let me introduce my country to you
It has four large islands
And many small ones –
More than six thousand!

Red and white – that's our flag
Green and blue – a land so beautiful..

Ours is a culture so special
Both modern and traditional

Our costume is the "Kimono"
Filled with design, so charming!

Have you ever seen "Sumo"?
It is our sport, so large and grand!

We love flowers and music
They make an atmosphere so unique!

We adore seafood
But dining in Japan is really expensive

Give us just a piece of paper
We can create a whole world
out of your notebook!

Whenever you are on a holiday
Do visit Japan!
All the best!

Japanese

Nihon ga daiski

Dedicated to my Japanese teacher Mrs. Fumiko Arai - the inspiration behind my career.

Sekai no ichiban ōki na
Umi no taiheiyō ni wa
Shizen ni tsukurareta yumi no yōni
Kireini mieru shimaguni

Doko wo mitemo utsukushii
Dareto attemo kimochi ii
Yūmeina yamamo kawamo kimo
Takusan aru nihon rettō

Jishin to kasan to taifū mo
Nihon no osoroshii koto;
Narete seikatsu suru Nihon no
Kino tsuyoi hitobito

Okanemochina shimaguni
Bunkamo yutakana kuni;
Genbakuni hakai saretanoni
Tsuyoku fukkatsu shita kuni

(Translation)

I love Japan

Amidst the Pacific,
The world's largest ocean,
One can see the island country -
Nature's own creation, shaped like a bow

Wherever you see, it's beauty
Whomever you meet, is friendly
This is Japan, an archipelago
With famous mountains, rivers and trees

Earthquakes, volcanoes and typhoons
Are Japan's nightmares;
Yet, they adapt and survive –
The brave-hearted people of Japan

A prosperous island country
With a rich culture
Though devastated by the atomic bomb,
She survived – by sheer will.

Hindi

Jab hum milen

Love – beyond the limits of time..

Jab hum milen...pehli baar...
Dil bhar tha, ye mera pyaar...
Sau saalon ka intezaar...
Ab bhi bhar hai, baar baar!

Mera deep hai, teri aankhon...
Mera sahara hai, teri baahon...
Tere dil se hai, meri sabdon...
Tere man se hai, meri sapnon...

Phool ke bina, kya Saavan...
Pyaar ke bina, kya Jeevan...
Dil ke bina, kya Bandhan...
Tere bina hai kya, mera man...

Saath hai hum, har janam...
Aajeevan bhi, O Sanam...
Ye sundar duniya ki kasam...
Haath se haath jodenge hum...

(Translation)

When we met for the first time
This love of mine filled my heart
It was a long wait of a hundred years..
But it still remains fresh..

Your eyes are my lamps
Your arms, my support
Fom your heart come my words
From your thoughts, my dreams..

What is spring without flowers
What is life without love
What is relationship without a heart
What am I, without you..

Every birth, we shall be together
For all those births yet to come, my dear
Let's promise, in the name of this beautiful world
That we shall always remain hand in hand..

Teri baahon mein

Towards heavenly bliss..with a beloved one..

Neel gagan mein, chand jaise
Mere man mein tu..
Baahon mein, teri aankon mein
Tere dil mein rehti hoon..
Sajna, tumse pyaar karoon..

Raste par phool aur kaante..
Phirbhi chale jaayen..
Zindagi bhar kushi aur gham hai..
Phirbhi reh jaayen..

Teri meri milan hai manzil
Roz ka sapna..
O tere bina jeena mushkil..
Akele kya karna..
Sajna, saat udjaayen..
Sajna, saat udjaayen..

(Translation)

Like the moon in the blue sky
You adorn my thoughts
I live in your eyes,
Your arms and your heart
Loving you all the time, my dear

There are flowers and thorns on our path
Yet we keep moving..
There is happiness and sadness in our lives
Yet we keep living..
Our meetings are our goals
The dreams of every single day

O my dear, life is difficult without you
What shall I do amidst this loneliness..
Let's fly away together..
O my love, let's fly away together..

Jaante ho?

Dreams bring us happiness and fulfill our wishes..
Sometimes, they become our real life..

Jaante ho,
Kyun main raath par aati hoon?
Tu hai mera aakaash ka chand..

Jaante ho,
Kyun tere sapnon mein aati hoon?
Sothe hue tere aankhen
Mujhe sunaate hain
Meri pyari, pyari kahani..

Jaante ho,
Kyun ithni kushi se naachti hoon?
Tera dil ki dhadkan hai
Meri Ghungroo ka swar..

Jaante ho,
Kyuun har raat aati hoon?
Neend mein aate hain
Hamaare pyare sapne..
Voh sapnon mein rahti hai
Hamari asli zindagi..

(Translation)

Do you know, why I come at night?
You are the moon of my skies..

Do you know, why I appear in your dreams?
To listen to those lovely stories your
sleeping eyes tell me..

Do you know, why I dance with such joy?
The beats of your heart
make the music of my anklets..

Do you know, why I come every night?
Sleep brings us our lovely dreams..
And in those dreams lies
Our real life..

Mousam

Monsoons are Indian favourites.. They inspire hearts in their own special way..

Kaala kaala baadal aaya
Thandi thandi baarish laaya
Achi mausam, aakaash ki maaya
piyo garm, garm chaaya (tea)

Nache log - tak dhim tak dhim
Varsha gaayee - rim jim rim jim
Garaj bolee - dhinak dhinak din
Khushi se man mein - ting ting ti ting!

(Translation)

Black rainclouds have arrived
Bringing cool showers along
Lovely weather..magic of the heavens
Enjoy your cup of hot tea!

People dance in joy
As the raindrops splatter
Thunder plays the beats
Oh, my heart leaps in delight!

Bhejo, na..

Letters are always special..be it handwritten ones or emails..

Sagar jaise neel hai, meri mail ki peti...
Ek lehar bhejo, na...
Gagan jaise neel hai, meri mail ki peti...
Ek chand bhejo, na...

(Translation)

My mailbox is blue
Like the wide, silent sea..
Please send me a (white) wave..

My inbox is blue
Like the vast, clear sky..
Please send me a (white) moon..

Taj Mahal

A friend once forwarded the picture of a multi-storeyed Taj Mahal – the eternal symbol of love. This poem uses the word multi-story, denoting the love legends associated with the architectural marvel.

Tere mere sapnon se
Chhoti, chhoti baaton se
Hum bhi banaenge
Ek aur (multi-story) Taj Mahal!

(Translation)

With dreams, yours and mine
With those sweet nothings
Let's too build
Another (multi-story) Taj Mahal!

Mutti mein

Longing for a nice chat with an extremely busy friend..

Akaash meri mutti mein..
Duniya bhi meri mutti mein..
lekin -
Tu meri mutti mein nahin!

(Translation)

The sky is within my reach..
Even the whole earth is within my reach..
But you –
Never!

Printed in the United States
By Bookmasters